Living in WALES

Annabelle Lynch

W
FRANKLIN WATTS
LONDON•SYDNEY

First published in 2014 by
Franklin Watts
338 Euston Road
London
NW1 3BH

Franklin Watts Australia
Level 17/207 Kent Street
Sydney
NSW 2000

HB ISBN 978 1 4451 2794 1
Library ebook ISBN 978 1 4451 2798 9

Dewey number: 942.9'08612
A CIP catalogue record for this book is
available from the British Library.

Series Editor: Julia Bird
Series Design: D.R. ink

Picture credits: Ammarhood/Dreamstime: 19t. APS(UK)/Alamy: 9b. Bob Brooky/Dreamstime: front cover b.
Blue Sky Image/Shutterstock: 12t. Clearvista/Dreamstime: 6b. Richard Cummins/Robert Harding PL: 8b.
Eldo/Shutterstock: 18b. Walter Galloway/istockphoto: 13c. Tatiana Gladskik/Shutterstock: front cover tcr, 8t.
Gpointstudio/Shutterstock: 16t. hansock/istockphoto: 13tc. Gail Johnson/Shutterstock: 5b, 11b, 19b. JTB Media Creation/
Alamy: 14b. Olga Khoroshunova/Dreamstime: 17t. Julius Kielaitis/Shutterstock: 5t. Scott Latham/Shutterstock: 7t.
Graham M Lawrence/Alamy: 20b. Richard M Lee/Shutterstock: 15b. Paul Matthew Photography/Shutterstock: 10t.
Monkey Business Images/Shutterstock: 15t. Jeff Morgan 10/Alamy: 21. Jeff Morgan 15/Alamy: 12b. Sergey Novikov/
Shutterstock: front cover tl. Patrimonio Designs/Dreamstime: 17b. peresanz/Shutterstock: 11t.
pio3/Shutterstock: front cover tcl, 4t. Steve Pleydell/Shutterstock: 10b. redsnapper/Alamy: 7b. Phil Rees/Alamy: 16b.
2xSamara.com/Shutterstock: front cover tr, 18t. Shestakoff/Shutterstock: front cover tlc, 14t. tirc83/istockphoto: 13tr.
Volodymyr Vyshnivetsky/Dreamstime: 20t. Christopher Ware/Dreamstime: 9t. Xanirakx/Shutterstock: 6t. Zurijeta/
Shutterstock: front cover trc.

Printed in China

Franklin Watts is a division of
Hachette Children's Books,
an Hachette UK company.
www.hachette.co.uk

Contents

Words in bold are in the glossary on page 23.

Welcome to Wales

Hello! I live in Wales. It is one of the four countries of the United Kingdom.

N **W** **E** **S**

Isle of Anglesey →

Llandudno

Bangor

Snowdonia

Irish Sea

WALES

Brecon Beacons

Swansea

Gower Peninsula →

Newport

CARDIFF

Bristol Channel

Wales in the UK

Wales is found to the west of the UK. It shares a long land **border** with England.

SCOTLAND

NORTHERN IRELAND

ENGLAND

WALES

Wales has more than 50 islands off its **coast**. The biggest island is called Anglesey.

A lighthouse on Anglesey.

North and south

Wales has lots of mountains, especially in the north and middle of the country. The big cities are mostly found in the south.

Weather

It rains a lot in Wales! In summer, the weather is usually warm. In winter it is mostly mild, although it does snow sometimes, especially in the mountains.

People in Wales

I was born in Wales. My grandparents came to live here from India.

Far and wide

Around three million people live in Wales today. Most people who live in Wales were born here, but some have come to live here from different countries in the UK. Other people living in Wales have moved here from as far away as Asia.

People at the seaside town of Llandudno in North Wales.

Travellers

People from Wales have settled in many other countries, including the USA and Australia.

A village in the **Welsh** valleys.

Where people live

Most people in Wales live in the south of the country, in and around the bigger cities. Fewer people live in the north and west of Wales, and in the countryside.

Different religions

Christianity has the most followers in Wales. Nearly two million people are Christian. The next biggest religious group are Muslims. There are around 50,000 Muslims in Wales. There are also many Hindus and Buddhists. Around 500,000 people don't follow any religion.

Many Muslims live in Wales.

Cities

I live in Cardiff, which is the **capital** *of Wales. Cardiff is the biggest city in Wales, and one of the largest cities in the UK.*

Important place

Lots of people come to Cardiff to work. Many businesses are based here. The Welsh **government** is also found here. Tourists come to visit Cardiff from all over the world.

Cardiff people

Around 350,000 people live in Cardiff and another 500,000 people live close to it.

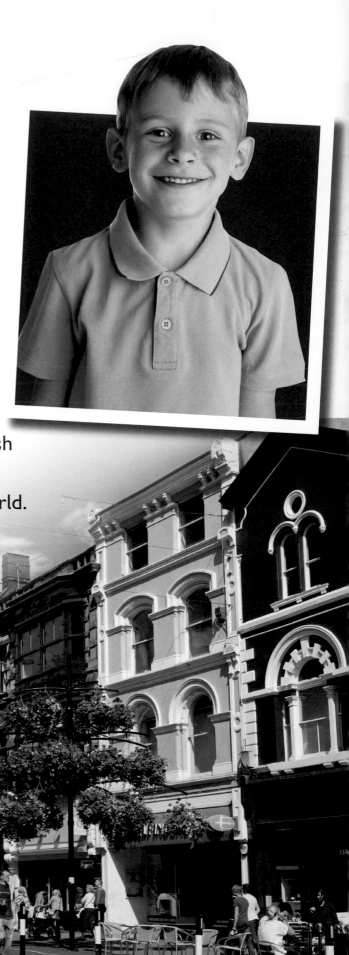

Cardiff Bay

Cardiff Bay used to be the busiest **port** in the world. It transported coal from Wales all over the world. Today it is still used for shipping, but it also has lots of flats, shops and cafés.

Other cities

Swansea is the second biggest city in Wales. It is by the sea and is very popular with tourists.

Other cities in Wales include Bangor in North Wales, and Newport.

Bangor is next to a stretch of water called the Menai Strait.

Coast and countryside

I live in the countryside of Wales. It is very beautiful here. Lots of people come to visit from other places.

Coast

Wales has a long coast. There are lots of wide, sandy beaches to play on and rocky **coves** to explore. Some of the best beaches are along the Gower Peninsula.

Three Cliffs Bay is on the Gower Peninsula.

Mountains

Some of the biggest hills and mountains in the UK are found in Wales. There are famous **national parks** in Snowdonia and in the Brecon Beacons. People go there to climb, hike and take in the amazing views!

Sky high

Mount Snowdon is the third highest mountain in the UK. It reaches up to a height of 1,085 metres.

Wildlife

You can see dolphins, whales and turtles off the Welsh coast. In the countryside there are many small animals including badgers and otters. Wild goats live in Snowdonia. And, of course, there are lots of sheep!

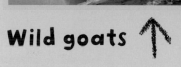

Wild goats ↑

The Welsh language

Everyone in Wales speaks English, but some people speak Welsh, too.

School

The Welsh language is called Cymraeg. About one in five people in Wales speaks it. Some people learn Welsh at home, but all children have Welsh lessons.

Signs and places

If you visit Wales, you'll see that some signs and place names are written in both English and Welsh. Some of the words look hard to say, but it's easy when you know how.

Big word

A village in Wales has one of the longest place names in the world — Llanfairpwllgwyngyllgogerychwyrndrobwllllantysiliogogogoch! (People call it Llanfair PG for short.)

Welsh words

Here are some useful Welsh words and phrases:

English	Welsh	How to say it
Hello	Helo	Hello
How are you?	Shw mae	Shoo-mai
Please	Plis	Please
Thank you	Diolch	Dee-olk
Good morning	Bore da	Boar-eh daa
Good night	Nos da	Noss daa
Goodbye	Hwyl	Who-ill

What we eat

We eat all kinds of food in Wales. Some dishes are the same as in other countries of the UK. Others are special to Wales.

← Laverbread

We often eat foods that come from the sea. One is laverbread. It isn't really bread though! It's actually seaweed mixed with oats and made into **patties**, which we fry and eat with bacon and eggs. It sounds strange, but it is really delicious.

New foods

Food in Wales is influenced by people coming to live here from other countries. The country's most popular dish is a curry called chicken tikka masala.

Cawl →

Lamb and leeks are two of the most famous foods to come from Wales. We put them together in a tasty stew called cawl, along with strips of bacon and other vegetables.

← Welsh cakes

Welsh cakes are like scones, but instead of baking them, they are cooked on a hot metal plate called a griddle. They are made with raisins and sometimes spices, and are covered in sugar.

Having fun

We love to have fun in Wales.
There is lot to do outdoors.
We also enjoy playing sport.

By the sea

When the weather is sunny, we head
to the beach to play and swim. If you're brave you can try
surfing or windsurfing, but you might want to take a **wet
suit** – the water's cold!

Outdoor fun

We also enjoy hiking, camping and biking in the countryside. Wales has some great trails for mountain biking.

Flying high

At Bethesda, near Bangor in North Wales, you can go on the longest zip wire in Europe!

Sport

Rugby is Wales' favourite sport, and we love to watch our national team play. We learn how to play rugby at school, and lots of people continue playing as adults. Football is also popular, both to watch and to play.

Famous places

Wales is a great place to visit. There are lots of exciting things to see.

Caerphilly Castle ↑

Wales has many old castles you can visit. Caerphilly Castle in South Wales is one of the biggest and most famous. You can climb to the top of its high towers, explore its mighty **gatehouses** and shiver in the spooky dungeon.

The Millennium Stadium ↑

The Millennium Stadium in Cardiff is where the Welsh rugby team play their matches. You can also see athletic events and concerts there. It has enough seats for 74,500 people!

Ffestiniog →

In the Snowdonia National Park, you can go on the famous Ffestiniog railway. It winds its way between the town of Porthmadog and the **mining** town of Blaenau Ffestiniog through over 20 kilometres of hills and forest.

Festivals and Special days

We celebrate lots of the same days as other countries in the UK, such as Christmas and Id. Some festivals are special to Wales, though.

Eisteddfod

Every summer, we celebrate Wales with the Eisteddfod festival. There are singing, dance and poetry competitions, and lots more to see and do. Everything is done in Welsh. Lots of people come to watch from all over Wales, as well as other countries.

Eisteddfod has some of the most famous singing competitions in the world.

Saint David's Day celebrations in Cardiff.

Saint David's Day

Saint David is the **patron saint** of Wales. We celebrate his day every year on 1 March. There are street **parades**, where people dress up in traditional Welsh clothes and hats. In schools, there are singing competitions. We often eat Welsh foods, such as cawl (see page 15). Everybody has fun!

Welsh flower

The daffodil is the national flower of Wales. People often wear daffodils on Saint David's Day.

Wales: Fast facts

Capital: Cardiff

Population: 3 million (2011)

Area: 20,779 sq km

Languages: Welsh, English

Currency: Pound sterling

Main religions: Christianity, Islam, Hinduism

Longest river: River Towy (121 km)

Highest mountain: Snowdon (1,085 m)

National holidays: New Year's Day (1 January), Good Friday, Easter Sunday, first Monday in May, last Monday in May, last Monday in August, Christmas Day (25 December), Boxing Day (26 December)

Glossary

border a line that divides two countries

capital the city in which the government of a country meets

coast where the land meets the sea

cove a small bay on the coast

gatehouse the building which surrounds a castle gate

government the group of people who run a country

mining to dig out materials, such as coal or precious metals, from under the Earth's surface

national park a protected area of countryside that people can visit

parade when a group of people walk or drive slowly through a place. Parades usually celebrate a special occasion

patron saint a holy person who is believed to look after a particular country or place. The patron saint of Wales is Saint David

patties small, flat cakes

port a place by the sea from where boats and ships arrive and depart

wet suit a costume made of a special material which keeps you warm in cold water

valley a low area of land between two hills

Index